The SCIENCE BEHIND the ATHLETE

# GOLF

India James

A Crabtree Crown Book

Crabtree Publishing

# School-to-Home Support for Caregivers and Teachers

This appealing book is designed to teach students about core subject areas. Students will build upon what they already know about the subject, and engage in topics that they want to learn more about. Here are a few guiding questions to help readers build their comprehensions skills. Possible answers appear here in red.

## Before Reading:

*What do I know about golf?*

- *I know golf is a sport.*
- *I know golf is played with clubs and balls.*

*What do I want to learn about this topic?*

- *I want to know what the first golf balls were made of.*
- *I want to learn how science is helping to conserve natural resources on golf courses.*

## During Reading:

*I'm curious to know...*

- *I'm curious to know how golf balls are made.*
- *I'm curious to know how golf clubs have changed.*

*How is this like something I already know?*

- *I know golf balls have dimples.*
- *I know golf clubs are made of metals.*

## After Reading:

*What was the author trying to teach me?*

- *The author was trying to teach me how technology is used while playing golf.*
- *The author was trying to teach me how math is used in golf.*

*How did the photographs and captions help me understand more?*

- *The photographs helped me understand how science has improved golf.*
- *The captions gave me extra information about the history of golf.*

# TABLE OF CONTENTS

# WHAT IS GOLF?

Golf is a game where players use different sized clubs to hit balls into a series of holes. Players win by using as few **strokes** as possible. Golf was first played in Scotland in the 1400s and is still very popular today.

## GOLF GUIDES

More than 50 million people worldwide play golf every year.

1

# GOLF CLUBS

The first golf clubs were made from wood. The **shaft** was made from ash or hazel trees. The **head** was made from apple, holly, beech, or pear trees.

## METAL HEADS

By the 1700s, iron and wood were used in the heads of clubs. This helped to make them stronger. Even with the stronger head, golf clubs often broke. Players often needed to replace their clubs, and golf clubs were expensive to make. Golf became a sport played by the wealthy.

## HEAD COVERING

Players experimented by covering the club head with different materials. They tried leather, fragments of bone, and different types of metal. Players hoped that these materials would prevent their clubs from breaking while helping them to hit the ball farther.

## GOING GROOVY

Grooves on the face of the head were introduced in 1908. Players discovered that these grooves helped the ball travel farther.

### GOLF GUIDES

In the early 1900s, most players carried 20-30 clubs with them when they played. In 1939, a rule was created that limited each player to only 14 clubs.

## NEW MATERIALS

Players continued trying golf clubs made of different materials. They experimented with fiberglass, graphite, synthetic, and composite materials.

## OVERSIZED HEAD

One of the most popular developments was an oversized club head. The bigger size helps players hit the ball farther. The bigger head also means there is more space on the club to hit the ball. This gives players a better chance of connecting with the ball.

### GOLF GUIDES

Oversized heads weren't popular until 1991 when the golf company Callaway introduced its club named Big Bertha.

# 2 GOLF BALLS

The first games of golf were played with balls made from wood. By the end of the 1400s, balls filled with cow's hair or straw and covered with leather were more popular.

*Old wooden golf ball*

## THE FEATHERIE

Around 1618, players discovered that balls could be packed more tightly if they were filled with goose or chicken feathers. These were called "featherie" balls. They were made with wet feathers and wet leather. The feathers expanded as they dried. The leather shrank as it dried. This made a harder ball than those stuffed with straw or cow's hair.

It took a long time to make featherie balls, and the materials were expensive. The balls also broke after a few uses. They fell apart if they got wet. This meant that players needed to have a lot of golf balls.

*Featherie balls*

The featherie ball was used for more than two centuries. Then, in the 1800s, two designs changed the golf ball forever.

*This 1887 illustration from a golfing handbook shows the game of golf from the time.*

## THE GUTTIE

The Gutta-Percha ball, or Guttie, was invented in 1848. It was made from the **sap** of the Malaysian sapodilla tree. The sap could be easily **molded**, and even remolded when the ball was damaged.

### GOLF GUIDES

The Guttie was the first ball to be made with marks on the surface. Players found that their balls went farther after they had damage to the surface. They began to hit new balls with hammers to **replicate** this damage. The dimples on golf balls today have the same effect.

## RUBBER-CORE GOLF BALL

The rubber-core golf ball was invented in 1898. This is the basis for golf balls used today. Layers of different material are built up around a bouncy core. Different materials and different layers create balls that fly farther or spin more in the air.

### GOLF GUIDES

Exactly how golf balls are made today is kept secret. Top manufacturers each use different materials and different methods to develop slightly different golf balls.

# 3 GOLF CARTS

For most of the history of golf, players walked the **course**. A **caddie** would carry their equipment so that players could concentrate on the game. Caddies also help players decide which club to use.

## EARLY GOLF CARTS

The first powered golf carts were used in the 1930s. They ran on electric batteries. Sometimes these carts needed six different batteries just to complete one course. Most people continued to walk while playing golf instead of using a cart.

### GOLF GUIDES

Most people call them golf carts, but the official term is golf cars. This is because these vehicles are self-propelled, or able to move by their own power. A cart is something pushed or pulled by humans or animals.

## BATTERIES

Batteries improved in the 1950s. Carts could complete several rounds of an 18-hole course on one charge. This made them more appealing to players. Golf carts quickly grew popular.

## GOLF CARTS TODAY

Golf cart design hasn't changed much since the 1950s. Most golf carts are electric and can complete seven or eight rounds of an 18-hole course without needing to be recharged.

### GOLF GUIDES

A typical golf cart today weighs around 950 pounds (431 kg), and is about 8 feet (2.4 m) long, 4 feet (1.2 m) wide, and 6 feet (1.8 m) high. It is made to hold two people and their clubs.

Golf carts today can do a lot more than just take players from hole to hole. Computers on some golf carts can give players important information about the course. Video displays can show the upcoming hole and give information about how to set up for the next shot.

## GOLF GUIDES

There is a large market for golf carts for people who do not play golf. Older people may use them to get around retirement communities and may decorate and customize their carts.

# 4 GOLF COURSES

Every golf course has a different design. Different landscapes made of grassy areas, water features, forests, elevation changes, and sand traps help to create the character of each course.

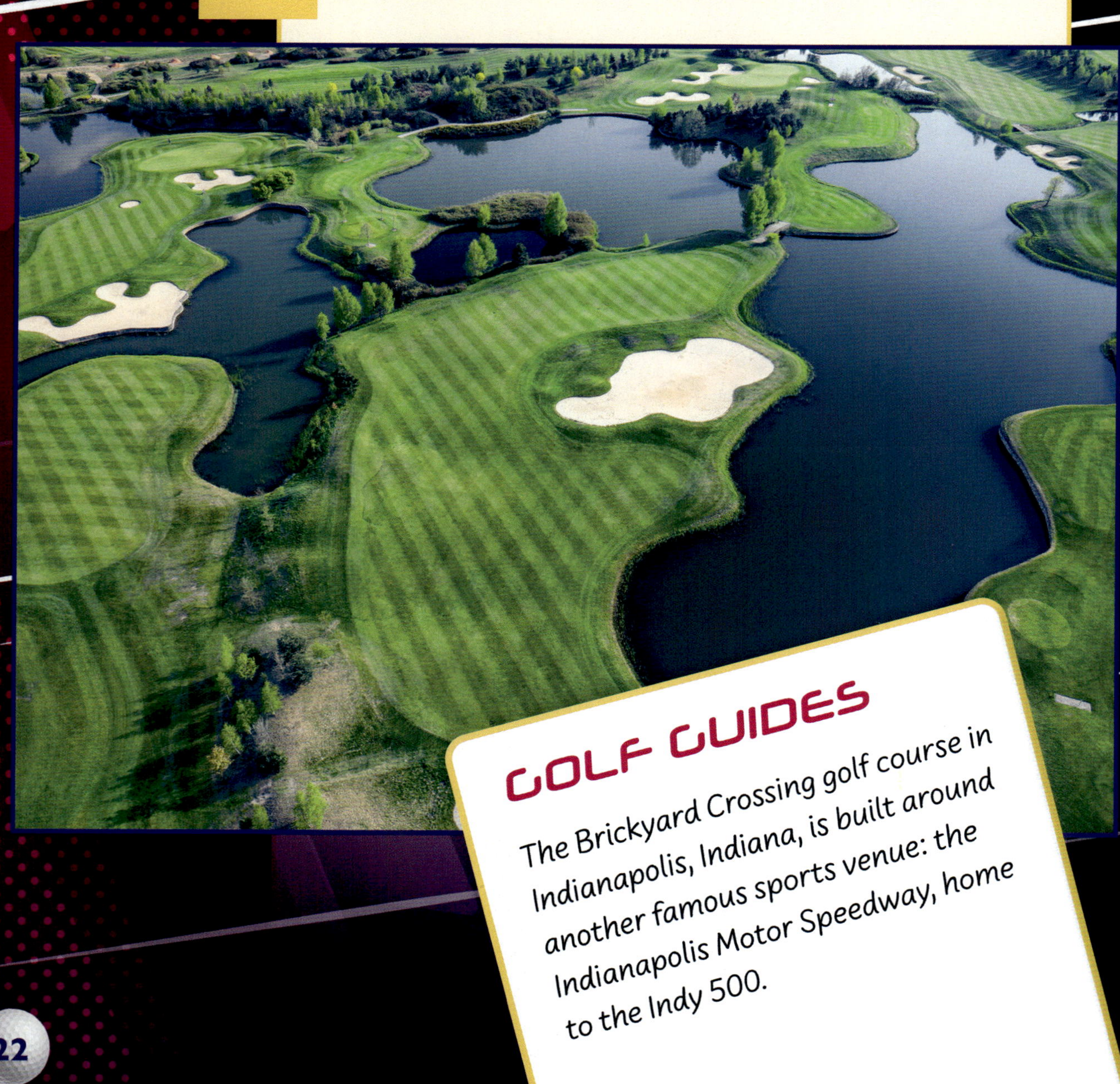

## GOLF GUIDES

The Brickyard Crossing golf course in Indianapolis, Indiana, is built around another famous sports venue: the Indianapolis Motor Speedway, home to the Indy 500.

Taking care of each of these courses is a lot of work. Technology helps make this job easier.

## ROBOTIC MOWERS

Robotic mowers may be used to trim the grass on putting greens. The robot can cut precisely, giving the putting green the crisp border that golfers need.

## DRONES

**Drones** also help maintain golf courses. By flying above a golf course, drones help to identify areas that need attention. Some drones can also be programmed to fly the same routes every day.

## DROUGHT

Drones are especially important in areas where drought is a concern. Areas with drought have very little water. Providing extra water and care to only the areas of a golf course that need it helps to limit the amount of water used to take care of a course. Using as little water as possible helps conserve this natural resource for other uses.

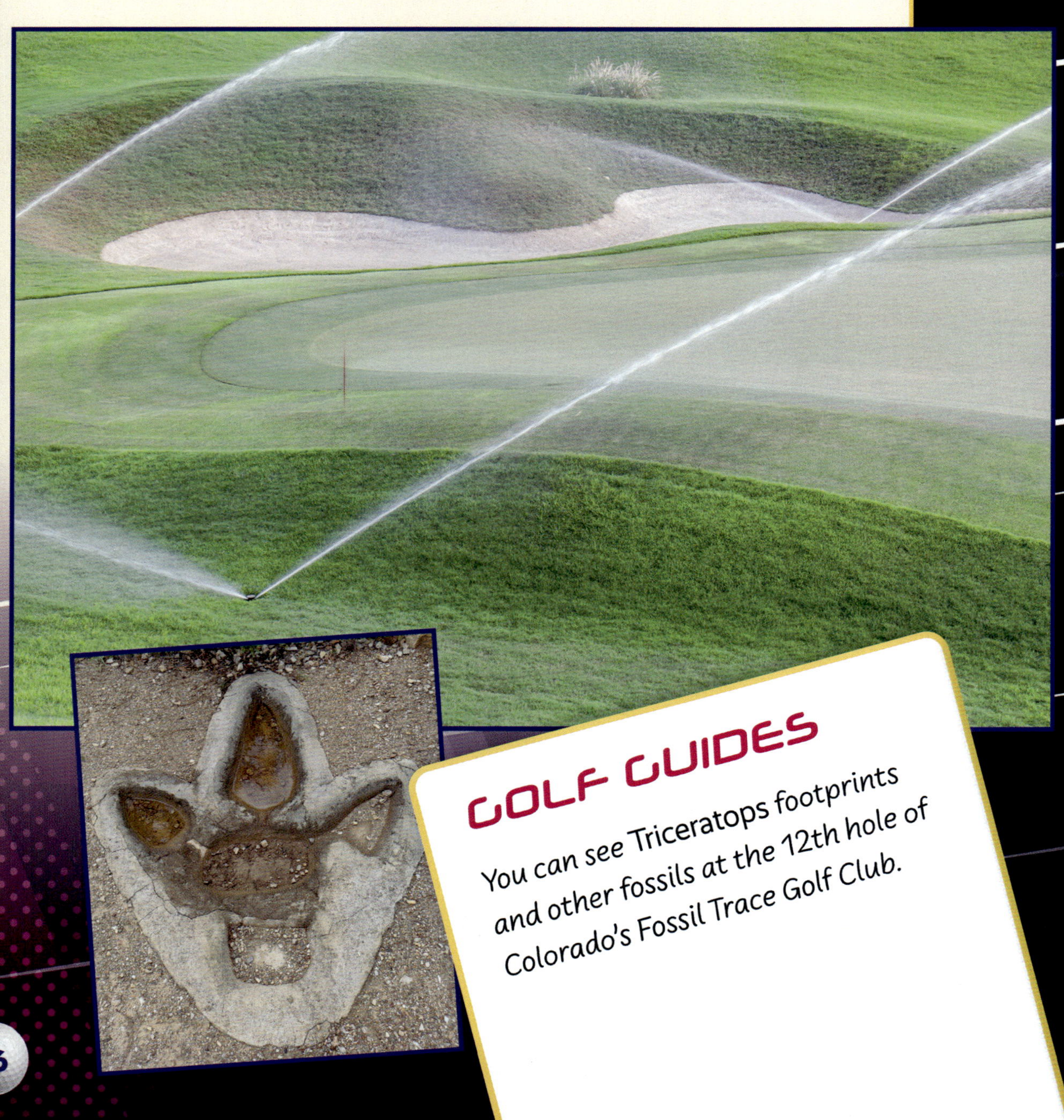

### GOLF GUIDES

You can see Triceratops footprints and other fossils at the 12th hole of Colorado's Fossil Trace Golf Club.

5

# STATISTICS

Hitting the ball might be the most exciting part of the game, but golf is a sport that depends a lot on math. **Statistics** is one area where math is used to help understand the game.

## STATISTICS

Statistics is an area of math that collects, organizes, and **analyzes** sets of numbers. In golf, statistics are used to explain how players are performing and how well they're hitting the ball. Coaches, scouts, and the media all use statistics to understand how players are performing.

*Players keep track of how many strokes they needed for each hole. Even recreational players can calculate their own statistics.*

## STATISTICS IN GOLF

Drive distance measures how far a player first hits a ball. Drive accuracy measures how often a player hits the **fairway** with their first shot. Strokes gained describes how many strokes a player needed to finish a course compared to other players. This helps a player identify areas where they can improve their game.

# CONCLUSION

The game of golf is a sport that has been around for centuries. Clubs, balls, carts, and course maintenance have changed since the first time golf was played. Science and technology can help make the sport more exciting and the equipment better in the future.

# GLOSSARY

**analyze** (AN-uh-lize): To examine carefully and in detail

**caddie** (KAD-ee): A person who carries a golf player's clubs on a golf course

**course** (kohrs): An area of land that is used for playing golf. A golf course can be nine or 18 holes.

**drone** (drohn): A type of small aircraft that is remotely operated and usually has video or picture cameras

**fairway** (FAIR-wey): An area of a golf course where the grass is cut even and short, between where a golfer first hits the ball and the hole

**head** (hed): The part of the golf club that is used to hit the ball

**mold** (mohld): To form something into a particular shape

**replicate** (REP-li-keyt): To copy something exactly

**sap** (sap): The liquid part of a plant or tree that carries nutrients

**shaft** (shaft): The long, narrow part of the golf club that players hold

**statistics** (stuh-TIS-tiks): A branch of math that collects, organizes, and analyzes numbers

**stroke** (strohk): A swing of the golf club made to hit the ball

# INDEX



# COMPREHENSION QUESTIONS

1. When was golf first played?
   a. 1000s
   b. 1400s
   c. 1900s
2. Which material was used in the first golf balls?
   a. wood
   b. rocks
   c. flour
3. What is an example of a statistic measured in golf?
   a. jump height
   b. timed 100-yard dash
   c. drive accuracy
4. **True or False:** Math is important in golf.
5. **True or False:** Golf club heads have always been the same size.

**Answers:** 1. B, 2. A, 3. C, 4. True, 5. False

# ABOUT THE AUTHOR

**India James** writes about science, technology, and math for young readers. She loves when science comes together with sports. India lives in Ohio with her family.

Written by: India James
Designed by: Kathy Walsh
Series Development: James Earley
Proofreader: Melissa Boyce
Educational Consultant: Marie Lemke M.Ed.

Photographs: Shutterstock; Cover & Title pg: Scott W. Grau/Icon SportswireviaNewscom, Lilo Alfonso, geen graphy, your; p 2-31 backgrounds: Lilo Alfonso, your; pg numbers: grey_and; p 4: Torwaistudio; p 5: titelio; p 6: @Wiki; p 7: aastock; p 8: Paul Dempsey, Vincent Giordano Photo; p 9: Daniela Pelazza; p 10: Belinda Pretorius; p 11: Photo Melon; p 12: Hitdelight, Alex Jackson; p 13: @Wiki; p 14: Anne Greenwood; p 15: @Wiki, Goodly Pixels; p 16: Annop Kesorn, FotoFeast; p 17: Chen WS; p 18: Ljupco Smokovski, Library of Congress; p 19: PxHere; P 20: Lucky Business; p 21: Andrio, Jillian Cain Photography; p 22: Curioso.Photography; p 23: Microgen; p 24: OrthsmedienGmbH, tonkid; p 25: Romsvetnik, AP_studio; p 26: mrcmos, laura camila barbosa; p 27: sirtravelalot; p 28: EpicStockMedia, Dennis Sabo; p 29: SujinKim

**Crabtree Publishing**

crabtreebooks.com 800-387-7650



Printed in Canada/012024/CP20231127

**Published in Canada**
**Crabtree Publishing**
616 Welland Ave.
St. Catharines, Ontario
L2M 5V6

**Published in the United States**
**Crabtree Publishing**
347 Fifth Ave
Suite 1402-145
New York, NY 10016

**Library and Archives Canada Cataloguing in Publication**
Available at Library and Archives Canada

**Library of Congress Cataloging-in-Publication Data**
Available at the Library of Congress

Hardcover: 978-1-0398-3897-0
Paperback: 978-1-0398-3982-3
Ebook (pdf): 978-1-0398-4056-0
Epub: 978-1-0398-4128-4